Slave Spirituals and the Jubilee Singers

Slave Spirituals and the Jubilee Singers

Michael L. Cooper

Clarion Books / New York

To Jim Giblin

Clarion Books
a Houghton Mifflin Company imprint
215 Park Avenue South, New York, NY 10003
Copyright © 2001 by Michael L. Cooper

The text was set in 12-point Giovanni Book.

For information about permission to reproduce selections
from this book, write to Permissions, Houghton Mifflin Company,
215 Park Avenue South, New York, NY 10003.

www.houghtonmifflinbooks.com

Printed in U.S.A.

Library of Congress Cataloging-in-Publication Data

Cooper, Michael L., 1950-
Slave spirituals and the Jubilee Singers / by Michael Cooper.
p.   cm.
ISBN 0-395-97829-7
1. Spirituals (songs)—History and criticism—Juvenile literature. 2. African Americans—
Music—Juvenile literature. 3. Jubilee Signers. [1. Spirituals (Songs) 2. African
Americans—Music. 3. Jubilee Singers. 4. African Americans—Biography.] I. Title.

ML3556.C67 2001
782.42162'96073'00922—dc21   00-065854

CRW   10   9   8   7   6   5   4   3   2   1

Acknowledgments

Special thanks to Barbara Bader, whose talk in 1998 at the Children's
Book Guild of Washington, D.C., inspired this book. Special thanks also
to Mrs. Beth M. Howse, Reference Librarian, Fisk University Library; to
Ginger Mauler at the Picture Collection of the Library of Virginia; and to
Michael J. Winey, Curator, U.S. Army Military History Institute.

Contents

Foreword

"Michael, Row the Boat Ashore," "Swing Low, Sweet Chariot," "Go Down, Moses," and "Steal Away to Jesus" are just some of the popular songs known as spirituals. Many people today enjoy singing these old songs. But there was a time when they were sung only by American slaves, who often had to sing in secret because the meaning of their songs frightened their owners.

African American intellectuals have long recognized the significance of this music. The novelist Richard Wright observed that slaves "left a vivid record of their sufferings and longings in those astounding religious songs known as the spirituals."

According to Eileen Southern, a professor at Harvard University: "Music was a primary form of communication for the slaves, just as it had been for their African forebears. Through the medium of song the slaves could comment on their problems and savor the few pleasures allowed them; they could voice their despair and hopes, and assert their humanity in an environment that constantly denied their humanness. As in the African tradition, the songs of the slaves could tell their history and reveal their everyday concerns."

And the poet and writer James Weldon Johnson, who compiled two collections of spirituals in the 1920s, wrote: "In many of the Spirituals the Negro gave wide play to his imagination; he dreamed his dreams and declared his visions; he uttered his despair and prophesied his victories; he also spoke the group wisdom and expressed the group philosophy of life. Indeed, the Spirituals taken as a whole contain a record and a revelation of the deeper thoughts and experiences of the Negro in this country for a period beginning three hundred years ago and covering two and a half centuries. If you wish to know what they are you will find them written more plainly in these songs than in any pages of history."

As these scholars and writers understood, American slaves created some of the world's most moving music. But the songs of these unlettered and unread people were not always widely appreciated. They had to be discovered. People first started writing down the words to spirituals during the Civil War.

1

Strange and Beautiful Songs

When Colonel Thomas Wentworth Higginson heard his soldiers singing "Many Thousand Go," he quickly took a pencil and a piece of paper from his jacket pocket and wrote down the words:

> *No more peck of corn for me,*
> *no more, no more.*
> *No more peck of corn for me,*
> *many thousand go.*
> *No more driver's lash for me,*
> *no more, no more.*
> *No more driver's lash for me,*
> *many thousand go.*

The soldiers, dressed in new blue uniforms of the Union army, were African Americans recently freed from slavery. These men were always singing. Their favorite song was the popular Civil War tune "John Brown's Body," but they knew dozens of others that Colonel Higginson had never heard before. The music fascinated the colonel, and he was one of the first people to write down the old slave songs.

"My interest," Higginson explained, "was rather increased by the fact that I had for many years heard of this class of songs under the name of 'Negro spirituals,' and had even heard some of them sung by friends from South Carolina. I could now gather on their own soil these strange plants."

The U.S. Army assigned Higginson, a thirty-nine-year-old Massachusetts native, to Port Royal, South Carolina, in February 1862, to command the First South Carolina Volunteers. The eight hundred soldiers in his regiment were the first newly freed slaves to serve in the Union army. They were guarding Port Royal Island, deep within Confederate territory. The Union army had captured Port Royal and several other large islands, which are part of a chain called the Sea Islands, just south of Charleston, South Carolina. This invasion had come only seven months after rebellious Southerners fired on Fort Sumter in Charleston Harbor and started the Civil War.

The day of the Union invasion, November 7, 1861, most of the white people living on the Sea Islands fled inland, leaving behind their plantations as well as some ten thousand slaves. Union generals coerced many of the former slaves into the army. They also hired black laborers to build docks for a naval station on neighboring Hilton Head Island to supply Union ships blockading Confederate ports on the Atlantic coast from Virginia down to Florida. The army confiscated the islands' large plantations and their cotton crops. The U.S. government could sell the fiber to textile mills in the North and earn millions of dollars to help pay for the war.

The American Missionary Association (A.M.A.) and other northern antislavery organizations recruited young men and women from Boston, New York, and Philadelphia to live in the Sea Islands and manage the government's plantations as well as establish schools for the former slaves. Because many of these young Northerners were sponsored by churches, they were nicknamed Gideon's Band, or Gideonites.

In their letters to friends and families, the Gideonites described the beautiful subtropical Sea Islands, their white sand beaches, the palmettos, and the live oak trees draped with wispy gray Spanish moss. They wrote with contempt about the planters who had lived comfortably in big plantation houses filled with expensive European furniture, while their slaves lived nearby in one-room shacks. The Northerners were most fascinated, though, by the black Sea Islanders: how they lived, what they thought, and, especially, their unique songs.

While traveling by wagon across Port Royal Island, one Gideonite stopped to listen to a group of men and women singing as they worked. "Sixty-eight hands in the potato field planting sweet potatoe, swing their hoes in unison," the man noted, "timed by a jolly song, words indistinguishable."

The African Americans not only sang as they worked, they also celebrated important events with song. The Northerners held a large Fourth of July celebration in 1862, and hundreds of African Americans sang the old slave spiritual "Roll, Jordan, Roll." One spectator reported: "The singing was intrinsically good. The song is strange and beautiful; and their swaying to and fro had a sort of oceanic grandeur to it."

Colonel Thomas Wentworth Higginson was one of the first people to write down slave spirituals. U.S. Army Institute of Military History

Newly freed slaves near Port Royal, South Carolina THE NEW-YORK HISTORICAL SOCIETY

Colonel Higginson often questioned his soldiers about their singing. "I asked one of the blacks—one of the most intelligent of them—where they got these songs." The colonel was referring to Prince Rivers, a sergeant in the First South Carolina Volunteers. Rivers, a former coachman, explained how slaves created songs like "Many Thousand Go."

"'Dey make em, sah. I'll tell you, it's dis way. My master calls me up and order me a short peck of corn and a hundred lash. My friends see it, and is sorry for me. When dey come to the praise meeting dat night dey sing about it. Some's very good singers and know how dey work it in—work it in, you know, tell they get it right. And dat's de way.'"

Other soldiers offered similar explanations. "Some good spiritu-als are start jess out o' curiosity," explained one man who described how he and several friends composed a song about a driver, or fore-man, who had been working them too hard. "Once we boys went for tote some rice and de nigger-driver he keep a-calling on us; and I say, 'O de ole nigger-driver!' Den annuder said, 'Fust ting my mammy tole me was, notin' so bad as nigger-driver.' Den I made a sing, just puttin' a word, and den anudder word."

> *O, de ole nigger-driver!*
> *O, gwine away!*
> *Fust ting my mammy tell me,*
> *O, gwine away!*
> *Tell me 'bout de nigger-driver,*
> *O, gwine away!*
> *Nigger-driver second devil,*
> *O, gwine away!*
> *Best ting for do he driver,*
> *O, gwine away!*
> *Knock he down and spoil he labor,*
> *O, gwine away!*

One of the regimental drummer boys told Colonel Higginson that slaves had to be careful about singing some songs around white people.

> *We'll fight for liberty*
> *Till de Lord shall call us home;*
> *We'll soon be free*
> *Till de Lord shall call us home.*

"This is the hymn which the slaves at Georgetown, South Carolina, were whipped for singing when President Lincoln was elected," noted Higginson. "So said a little drummer boy . . . 'Dey tink "de Lord" meant . . . de Yankees.'"

But the Gideonites sometimes disapproved of the slaves' music as well, and nearly all white people seemed to dislike a practice called a "shout." This was a long ritual, often lasting for hours, of singing and dancing that lulled participants into a trance. No one knows exactly why slaves called this form of ring dancing a shout. One visitor described the long, strange dance, which he believed was "purely African in form and tradition.

"The constant and ever-repeated refrain of some familiar hymn would bring up the dances, and to the accompaniment of a 'regular drumming of the feet and clapping of the hands,' they would circle about, 'winding monotonously round something in the centre' while the excitement and intensity of the dance spread. . . . Some 'heel and toe,' tumultuously, others merely tremble and stagger on, others stop and rise, others whirl, others caper sideways, all keep steadily circling like dervishes."

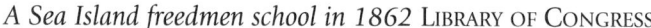

A Sea Island freedmen school in 1862 LIBRARY OF CONGRESS

Soldiers of the First South Carolina Volunteers celebrated the Emancipation Proclamation on January 1, 1863, with music and singing. SOUTH CAROLINA HISTORICAL SOCIETY

"I never saw anything so savage," one teacher wrote. It was the "most hideous and at the same time the most pitiful sight I ever witnessed." Another Northerner believed the shout was "handed down by African ancestors and destined to pass away under the influence of Christian teachings." Despite the disapproval of white people, slaves continued to hold shouts secretly.

The shout was not the only sign of the exslaves' African heritage. A few of the Sea Islanders had been born in Africa, and they told stories about their faraway homeland. Monday, an elderly man with a tattoo on his forehead that identified his clan, said his older brother had sold him to a slave trader in order to pay a debt. Maum Katie entertained children with stories about spirits and magical creatures she had learned long ago as a girl in Africa. Sea Island blacks like Monday and Maum Katie spoke a unique language called Gullah, a mix of African and English words unintelligible to outsiders. Enslaved African Americans used remnants of their old languages and customs in their everyday lives. And music was the most important of the African customs to survive among the slaves.

Today slave spirituals are familiar to people the world over. But back in 1862, when Colonel Higginson and the Gideonites first collected these songs, they sounded new and strange. Many people wondered how illiterate people in bondage could create such music.

Musical Africa

American slaves like Monday and Maum Katie came from Africa, where music and dancing are important in daily life. "We are almost a nation of dancers, musicians, and poets," observed Olaudah Equiano, an Ibo man from the Kingdom of Benin in West Africa. "Thus every great event such as a triumphant return from battle or other cause of public rejoicing is celebrated in public dances, which are accompanied by songs and music suited to the occasion."

The African continent, which is nearly three times as large as the United States, is home to many different nations and traditions. Most slaves brought to America came from western Africa, a large region that today includes such countries as Cameroon, Congo, Guinea, Ivory Coast, Nigeria, Senegal, Togo, and Democratic Republic of the Congo. American slaves also represented a variety of clans, including Wolof, Ibo, Ashanti, Bakongo, and Mandingo. Yet amid all this diversity, African people shared many similarities.

Early European travelers often commented upon the prevalence of music among the Africans. "There is without doubt," wrote an English sea captain visiting the continent in 1620, "no people on the earth more naturally affected [by] the sound of musicke than these people." The Europeans noticed that African music was very different from their own.

Traders in Africa buying captives to sell to slave ships bound for the New World
Library of Congress

African men and women sang songs for all of life's milestones, such as childbirth, marriage, and death. They used songs to teach children their clans' customs and beliefs. Africans also sang work songs while fishing, boating, gardening, cooking, and selling goods at market. Lyrics and melodies were not written down, so adults had to remember hundreds of tunes.

Some villages maintained professional orchestras and song leaders. The instruments in the orchestras included drums, flutes, horns, rattles, and a variety of stringed instruments. African craftsmen made horns and trumpets from elephant tusks and animal horns. They made flutes, fiddles, harps, lyres, and zithers from hollow reeds, gourds, and tree branches, using fibrous roots or cow hair for strings. Craftsmen made small drums and rattles from gourds and large drums from hollowed-out logs. Priests and kings used these instruments in their sacred and royal ceremonies. The Africans also used drums to communicate over long distances. Skilled drummers pounded various combinations of rhythms and pitches, sending messages quickly from village to village.

Professional song leaders, like choir directors, led the singing during public ceremonies. The song leader, using a technique known as call and response, or lining, called out the lyrics to unfamiliar songs, one line at a time, and the crowd sang them back. African singers surprised Europeans with their complex rhythms and their wide variety of vocal techniques, including shouts, groans, guttural tones, and falsetto singing.

Dancing was another important part of African life. Individuals and whole villages danced for recreation and communication. At public dances spectators sang refrains, clapped their hands, tapped their feet, shouted encouragement to the dancers, and jumped in and out of the dance ring. African dance both fascinated and disgusted European visitors, who were accustomed to stiffer styles of dancing. G. T. Basden, an English traveler, described a public dance he saw in Nigeria.

"The dancers range themselves and begin slow rhythmic movements, unconsciously swaying their heads in time with the music. As the dance proceeds they appear intoxicated with the motion and the music, the speed increases, and the movements become more and more intricate and bewildering. . . . The twistings, turnings, contortions and springing movements, executed in perfect time, are wonderful to behold. . . . For these set dances . . . the physical strength required is tremendous. The body movements are extremely difficult and would probably kill a European."

Africans frequently improvised, or made up on the spot, lyrics and melodies as they sang or played their instruments. African men and women quickly improvised songs to describe their feelings or simply to describe an event. This improvisation was observed by Mungo Park, a late-eighteenth-century Scottish explorer who spent several years traveling in Africa.

Park arrived at a village hoping to find shelter and food. People elsewhere had been hospitable, but residents of this village avoided him. As evening neared and a storm gathered, a woman took pity on Park. She invited the Scotsman to her house and gave him food and a mat to sleep on. The woman and several friends stayed up most of the night, spinning cotton and singing a song that she had made up about her visitor. Park understood much of what the woman was singing, and he wrote down the words. This is one of the earliest known examples of an African song translated into English or any European language.

> *The winds roared and the rains fell;*
> *The poor white man, faint and weary,*
> *Came and sat under our tree.*
> *He has no mother to bring him milk,*
> *No wife to grind his corn.*
>
> *Let us pity the white man*
> *No mother has he to bring him milk,*
> *No wife to grind his corn.*

Africans forced into bondage by hostile tribes or by Europeans carried their musical customs with them to the New World.

The slave ships sailed from Africa across the Atlantic Ocean to the Americas. This journey, called the Middle Passage, took from three weeks to three months. The ships' captains kept the "cargo," hundreds of men and women, in dark and cramped holds. The crew brought the Africans up on deck once or twice a day for exercise, which often consisted of singing and dancing.

Conditions down in the ship's hold were terrible. One captain described the scene during a storm, when the portholes were closed and fever had spread among the men and women below. "The floor of their rooms was so covered with the blood and mucus which has

The crowded hold of a slave ship during the Middle Passage LIBRARY OF CONGRESS

proceeded from them in consequence of the flux, that it resembled a slaughterhouse." One out of every five Africans died during the journey.

Survivors landed in the slave markets of the New World. Dutch, English, Portuguese, and Spanish slave traders brought an estimated ten million Africans to the Americas and sold them to plantations in their North American, South American, and Caribbean colonies. In the sixteenth, seventeenth, and eighteenth centuries the number of slaves and indentured servants brought to the New World outnumbered voluntary immigrants.

Olaudah Equiano, who was sold as a teenager to a Virginia plantation owner, expressed in a poem his feelings at being stolen from home.

The original frontispiece of Olaudah Equiano's autobiography LIBRARY OF CONGRESS

Well may I say my life has been
One scene of sorrow and of pain;
From early days I griefs have known,
And as I grew my griefs have grown.

Dangers were always in my path,
And fear of wrath and sometimes death;
While pale dejection in me reign'd
I often wept, my grief constrain'd.

When taken from my native land
By an unjust and cruel band,
How did uncommon dread prevail!
My sighs no more I could conceal.

Equiano and the millions of other slaves taken from a continent of dancers, musicians, and poets soon began to shape the music of their new homes.

3

Slave Music

Nearly four hundred years ago, in 1619, the first Africans arrived at Jamestown, Virginia. Over the following two centuries slave ships brought many more Africans—an estimated 600,000—to North America, where their music became part of daily life.

On holidays in colonial Pennsylvania and New York, slaves filled public squares to sing, dance, play banjos, and beat drums made of hides stretched over hollow logs. In the Quaker city of Philadelphia, a large crowd of African Americans gathered downtown, where Washington Square is today, to celebrate Pentecost Sunday. A hundred miles to the north, on the southern tip of Manhattan Island, thousands of slaves from nearby farms gathered in an open field, which is now City Hall Park. These holidays, which lasted as long as a week, were called Carnivals of the Africans, or Pinkster celebrations. The word *Pinkster* is believed to be derived from the word *Pentecost*.

Some of the biggest and most elaborate celebrations occurred on Albany's Pinkster Hill, where New York's state capitol building sits today. Dr. James Eights described a festival he saw as a child in Albany in the 1780s.

A prominent slave named Jackey Quakenboss played a large drum, Dr. Eights recalled, "beating lustily with his naked hands upon its loudly sounding head, successively repeating the ever wild,

The first nineteen slaves in the British colonies arrived in Jamestown, Virginia, in 1619. Library of Congress

though euphonic cry of Hi-abomba, bomba, bomba, a full harmony with the thumping sounds. These vocal sounds were readily taken up and as oft repeated by the female portion of the spectators not otherwise engaged in the exercises [dances] of the scene, accompanied by the beating of time with their ungloved hands."

Every Sunday in New Orleans, Louisiana, the big port city near the mouth of the Mississippi River, slaves streamed into Place Congo, the public square that is now Louis Armstrong Park, to spend the day singing and dancing. An onlooker one Sunday identified seven different African tribes—Kraels, Minahs, Congos, Mandringas, Gangas, Hiboas, and Fulas—among the hundreds of people in Place Congo. Men and women danced in large circles, slowly increasing the tempo until they fell exhausted to the ground. Slaves danced in New Orleans long after Pinkster celebrations in Philadelphia and New York had disappeared.

By the early nineteenth century every northern state had outlawed slavery, but in the South the institution grew rapidly, mainly because of the region's dependence on tobacco, cotton, and other types of agriculture. Cotton so dominated the South's economy by the mid-nineteenth century that people called it king—King Cotton. The region's plantations needed gangs of field hands to plant and harvest their large crops. When the Civil War began in 1861, the South's slave population, because of births and importation from the Caribbean, had grown to nearly four million people, about one third of the South's entire population.

Slaves wove their music into the fabric of everyday life. Southerners took for granted the constant singing of their slaves, but visitors from northern states and Europe found the singing unusual and wrote about it in their journals and letters.

Frederick Law Olmstead, the man who became famous for designing New York City's Central Park, described visiting a plantation and being awakened at dawn by slaves walking to the fields. "Suddenly one raised such a sound as I had never heard before; a long, loud musical shout, rising, and falling, and breaking into falsetto, his voice ringing through the woods in the clear, frosty night air, like a bugle-call. As he finished, the melody was caught up by another, and then, another, and then by several in chorus."

Martin Delany, an African American physician and newspaper editor who lived in Pittsburgh in the 1840s and 1850s, described the sounds he had heard on southern docks: "In the distance, on the levee and in the harbor among the steamers, the songs of the boatmen were incessant. Every few hours landing, loading and unloading, the glee of these men of sorrow was touchingly appropriate and impressive."

Hearing these songs led many people to believe African Americans were born with musical talent. Thomas Jefferson, the third president of the United States and himself a large slaveholder, felt blacks "are more generally gifted than the whites with accurate ears for tune and time." A magazine writer in 1856 informed his readers: "The Negro is a natural musician. He will learn to play on an instrument more quickly than a white man. They have magnificent voices and sing without instruction. . . . They go singing to their daily labors. The maid sings about the house, and the laborer sings in the field."

African Americans also believed they possessed special musical talents. "That's one thing the colored folks is blessed [with]," one unknown slave told an interviewer. "They certainly got the harp in their mouths."

Whites valued "bondsmen"—another word for slaves—who could sing, play a fiddle, or compose clever lyrics. Planters often summoned their talented bondsmen to entertain at parties or hired them out to neighboring plantations. A good fiddler or singer could escape his drab quarters and earn money as well. Being a professional musician became popular for both slaves and free blacks. Slaves played their instruments, sang, and danced for fun and, more importantly, to help ease the pain of bondage.

Solomon Northup, an educated free black man who had been kidnaped from his home in Saratoga Springs, New York, and sold into slavery in Louisiana, explained how his violin gave him comfort. "It was my companion—the friend of my bosom—triumphing loudly when I was joyful, and uttering its soft, melodious consolations when I was sad. Often, at midnight, when sleep had fled afrighted from the cabin, and my soul was disturbed and troubled with the contemplation of my fate, it would sing me a song of peace."

The violin, also known less formally as the fiddle, was a popular instrument in early America. Another popular instrument, believed to be African in origin, was the banjo. Slaves made banjos out of gourds and twine. Drums were also widely used among bondsmen until white Southerners learned to fear their sound.

In 1739 dozens of slaves revolted near Charleston, South Carolina. This revolt, which occurred near the Stono River, was called the Stono Rebellion. Slaves used drums to signal others to join them in killing whites. Local militias crushed the uprising and hanged dozens of the black rebels. In an attempt to prevent future revolts, southern officials banned drums. It was "absolutely necessary to the safety of this province," declared a Georgia law, "that slaves be prohibited from using and carrying mischievous and dangerous weapons, or using and keeping drums, horns, or other loud instruments, which may call together or give sign or notice to one another of their wicked designs and intentions."

The most common instrument available to every slave was his or her voice. Like the kind woman whom explorer Mungo Park met while traveling in Africa, bondsmen sang while working. "Slaves are generally expected to sing, as well as to work," observed Frederick Douglass, who grew up in slavery. "A silent slave is not liked by masters or overseers."

The songs, one planter explained, set the pace of the jobs being performed. "When at work I have no objection to their whistling or singing some lively tune, but no drawling tunes are allowed in the field, for their motions are almost certain to keep time with their music."

Like their African ancestors, slaves created songs for nearly every job. Music made their long days of working at repetitive tasks easier. One song, with the straightforward title of "Shuck That Corn," established a fast tempo while describing the rewards of the job.

> *All them pretty gals will be there,*
> *Shuck that corn before you eat;*
> *They will fix it for us rare,*
> *Shuck that corn before you eat.*
> *I know that supper will be big,*
> *Shuck that corn before you eat;*
> *I think I smell a fine roast pig,*
> *Shuck that corn before you eat.*

Workers sang this lively tune at corn shucking, or husking, parties. To get the job done quickly, the planter often borrowed some of his neighbors' slaves. The men and women joked, flirted, and held contests to see who could husk the most corn. Meanwhile, cooks prepared a feast to reward the workers.

Boats were an important means of transportation in early America, and slaves created many boat songs. One of the best known is "Michael, Row the Boat Ashore." The tune's slow tempo matched the rhythmic motions of men pulling the oars of a large boat.

Plantation slaves at a corn husking LIBRARY OF CONGRESS

Michael row de boat ashore, Hal-le-lu-jah!
Michael boat a gospel boat, Hal-le-lu-jah!
I wonder were my mudder deh [there].
See my mudder on the rock gwine home.
On de rock gwine home in Jesus' name.
Michael boat a music boat.
Gabriel blow de trumpet horn.
O you mind your boastin' talk.
Boastin' talk will sink your soul.
Brudder, lend a helpin' hand.
Sister, help for trim dat boat.
Jordan stream is wide and deep.
Jesus stand on t'oder side.
I wonder if my massa deh.
My fader gone to unknown land.
O de Lord he plant his garden deh.

The songs were versatile, and singers could change the tempo, substitute words, or add new verses. An old slave criticized young people for singing her favorite song, "Poor Rosy," too fast. They sang the words breezily, to match the speed of the gristmill grinding corn.

Poor Rosy, poor gal;
Poor Rosy, poor gal;
Rosy break my poor heart,
Heaven shall-a be my home;
I cannot stay in hell one day,
Heaven shall-a be my home.

"I likes 'Poor Rosy' better dan all the songs," the woman explained, "but it can't be sung widout a full heart and a troubled spirit."

African Americans made up songs not only to help them work but also to gripe about their neighbors, poke fun at white people, and express hope for escaping slavery. Slaves resisted bondage from the time the first European traders forced them onto ships in Africa. During the transatlantic voyage some flung themselves into the ocean to drown. In North America they ran away to live in swamps and forests. A few, such as the Stono rebels, rose up in armed insurrections against their masters. But the majority of enslaved Americans protested by small acts of defiance, which included singing. If white Southerners had understood their slaves' songs, they might have outlawed singing, just as they had outlawed drums and teaching bondsmen to read and write.

One man remembered a song he and other slaves sang about their stingy master. Plantation owners usually granted their servants and field hands a few days off from work at Christmas. It was a time for dancing, singing, and feasting. In eastern Virginia, planters customarily gave their bondsmen small gifts, such as coins, drinks of brandy, or pieces of cake. When this planter ignored the custom, his slaves made up a sarcastic song about him.

> *Poor massa, so dey say;*
> *Down in de heel, so dey say;*
> *Got no money, so dey say;*
> *Not one shillin', so dey say;*
> *God A'mighty bress you, so dey say.*

In another song slaves observed that they planted the gardens, raised the livestock, and cooked the meals—but received the worst food, such as the cooking water, called liquor, from boiled vegetables, while white people got the best.

> *We raise de wheat,*
> *Dey gib us de corn;*
> *We bake de bread,*
> *Dey gib us de crust;*
> *We sif de meal,*
> *Dey gib us de huss;*

We peel de meat,
Dey gib us de skin;
And dat's de way
Dey take us in;
We skim de pot,
Dey gib us de liquor,
And say dat's good enough for nigger.

Slaves used songs to comment on practically every aspect of their lives. It was common for slaves to roam about the countryside at night. Some were out to destroy plantation property by burning barns or poisoning farm animals. Others visited relatives and friends on neighboring plantations. And many attended secret religious meetings. To discourage such excursions, planters hired men to patrol the countryside. Patrollers beat slaves caught out after dark. In slave dialect these men were called patty rollers.

But if you don't mind, the patty roller catch you.
Massa was kind and Missus was true,
Run, nigger, run, for it's almost day.

Slave songs also gossiped about people's behavior. One song, "Roun' de Corn, Sally," was about a love affair.

Dere's Mr. Travers lub [love] Miss Jinny;
He thinks she is us good us any.
He comes from church wid her er Sunday
Un don't go back ter town till Monday.

Another song warned slaves against telling tales about their fellows to the overseer.

O' Judas he was a 'ceitful man,
He went and portray a mos innocen' man.
Fo' thirty pieces a silver dat it wuz done,
He went into the woods an' 'e self he hung.

24

One of the worst experiences for a slave—as well as for his family and friends—was to be sold. Jacob Stroyer, a South Carolina slave, described the sad scene when bondsmen who had been sold were being taken away. "Those who were going did not expect to see their friends again. While passing along many of the Negroes left their masters' fields and joined us . . . some were yelling and wringing their hands, while others were singing little hymns that they had been accustomed to for the consolation of those that were going away, such as,

> *When we all meet in heaven,*
> *There is no parting there,*
> *When we all meet in heaven,*
> *There is no parting there."*

A slave being sold LIBRARY OF CONGRESS

"Sold Off to Georgy," a slave song about a Virginia man whose master has sold him to faraway Georgia, describes the sad departure.

Farewell fellow sarvants!
O ho o ho.
I'm gwine way to leave you;
O ho o ho.
I'm gwine to leabe de ole county;
O ho o ho.
I'm sold off to Georgy;
O ho o ho.
My dear wife un one chile,
My poor heart is breaking;
No more shall I see you,
Oh, no more foreber!

Slaves who could be suddenly torn away from family and friends felt a profound sense of hopelessness. They shared common feelings of despair in songs such as "Sometimes I Feel Like a Motherless Child." The lyrics and the slow tempo of this song evoked a feeling every slave could immediately understand—the helplessness of an orphan, alone and unloved in the world. Such despair could cloud a bondsman's entire life, and many slaves sought hope and dignity in religion.

4

The Secret Church

A joke often told in the pre-Civil War South described a planter promising one of his slaves new boots if he would just sit quietly through an entire church service. The servant, who really wanted new boots, agreed. After listening silently to half the sermon, the bondsman jumped up and shouted, "Glory to God. Boots or no boots, glory to God."

As this joke suggests, white Southerners and slaves worshiped in different ways. White people, especially the wealthy planters, preferred quiet, solemn church services. And they wanted their servants to worship that way too. Slaves, on the other hand, felt very emotional during church services. "There is a joy on the inside and it wells up so strong that we can't keep still," an old bondsman explained. "It is fire in the bones. Any time that fire touches a man, he will jump."

African Americans liked to express their joy by singing, dancing, and shouting. Religion was so important to slaves that they often worshiped secretly. Away from disapproving white people, they freely combined old African customs of singing and dancing with Christian practices of praying and preaching.

Slaves enjoyed church services, commented William Channing Gannett, one of the Port Royal teachers, because, "Not only their soul but their mind finds here its principal exercise and in great measure it takes the place of social entertainment and amusements."

Many African Americans became Christians during two long periods of religious fervor, known as the Great Awakenings. The first Great Awakening started around 1740 and faded away in the 1760s. The next one, which historians call the Second Great Awakening, spanned the 1820s and 1830s. During both periods large crowds of people in cities, small towns, and frontier villages attended religious meetings called revivals.

In the Second Great Awakening there were as many as a thousand revivals a year, almost three a day. They were especially popular in the sparsely settled South and Midwest, where they were often called camp meetings because revivals were frequently held outdoors. Camp meetings gave farmers, villagers, and slaves opportunities to see friends and neighbors as well as to hear inspirational preaching. The outdoor revivals were not like traditional church services. Preachers dramatically strode across the stage, flailing their arms and yelling about good and evil, heaven and hell. Talented preachers kept crowds spellbound for hours, and revivals might last several days.

Singing was important at camp meetings. There were no hymnals for the large crowds, and besides, many of the people could not read. So the preacher or an assistant led the crowd in making up hymns from fragments of popular songs, familiar images from the Bible, and scenes of daily life. People began referring to these hymns as spirituals.

The camp meetings were popular among slaves. "I like a meetin' just as good as I like a party," said Julia Francis Daniels. Enthusiastic bondsmen sometimes dominated the singing. "A magnificent choir!" observed the Swedish novelist Fredrika Bremer, who attended a camp meeting in Georgia. "Most likely the sound proceeded from the black portion of the assembly, as their number was three times that of the whites, and their voices are naturally beautiful and pure."

Bremer described the scene: The slaves sang "with all their souls and with all their bodies in unison; for their bodies rocked, their heads nodded, their feet stamped, their knees shook, their elbows and their hands beat time to the tune and the words which they sang with evident delight. One must see these people singing if one is rightly to understand their life."

The itinerant preachers at the camp meetings were often Methodists or Baptists. They won many converts among slaves in the South during the Great Awakenings. Many planters were themselves religious and felt a duty to teach their bondsmen about Christianity and baptize them. To the modern mind it might seem contradictory for men who professed belief in God to own slaves. Yet whites viewed Africans as godless savages. Slavery, they claimed, benefited people of African heritage by introducing them to Christianity. The planters, or their wives, read the Bible to house servants and field hands, just as they would to their own children.

"Sunday was a great day around the plantation," recalled John Brown, a former slave. "The fields was forgotten, the light chores was hurried through, and everybody got ready for the church meeting. It was out of the doors, in the yard. . . . Master John's wife would start the meeting with a prayer and then would come the singing—the old timey songs."

White Southerners also took their slaves with them to church, where their singing was often admired. "I can hardly express the pleasure it affords me to turn to that part of the Gallery where they [slaves] sit," wrote the Reverend Samuel Davies, "all breaking out in a torrent of sacred harmony, enough to bear away the whole congregation to heaven."

Although blacks and whites attended the same churches, they criticized each other's style of worship. A white preacher voiced a common complaint: "[N]othing is more barbarous and contrary to Christianity, than their . . . idolatrous Dances, and revels; in which they usually spend Sunday."

Bondsmen were as critical, at least among themselves, of the ways white people preached and worshiped. Lucretia Alexander explained why she and other slaves disliked a white minister. "He just say, 'serve your masters. Don't steal your master's turkey. Don't steal your master's chickens. Don't steal your master's hawgs. Don't steal your master's meat. Do whatsomever your master tell you do to.' Same old thing all the time."

Cornelius Garner voiced a similar criticism. "Dat old white preacher jest was telling us slaves to be good to our marsters. We ain't keer'd a bit 'bout dat stuff he was telling us 'cause we wanted to sing, pray, and serve God in our own way."

A church service for slaves, with the master sitting conspicuously among his bondsmen
Library of Virginia

Free blacks at church in antebellum Cincinnati, Ohio LIBRARY OF CONGRESS

The desire to worship in their own way caused slaves to insist on separate church services. "Niggers commence to wanna go to church by de'selves, even ef dey had to meet in de white church," explained Sarah Fitzpatrick, an Alabama slave. "So white fo'ks have deir service in de mornin' an' Niggers have deirs in de evenin', a'ter dey clean up, wash de disches, an' look a'ter ever'thing. . . . Y'a see Niggers lack ta shout a whole lot an' wid de white fo'ks al' round 'em, dey couldn't shout jes' lack dey want to."

Religious slaves often prayed for freedom, and sometimes they even preached rebellion. And they expressed these and other forbidden feelings in their spirituals. "Every tone," observed Frederick

Douglass, "was testimony against slavery, and a prayer to God for deliverance from chains."

In the early nineteenth century black Americans, both slaves and the small population of free blacks, established their own separate churches in Charleston, South Carolina, Savannah, Georgia, and Lexington, Kentucky. But white officials eventually closed these churches because they suspected that the sermons fostered a rebellious spirit as well as a religious one.

Planters allowed their slaves to hold worship services in their own cabins or to build special "praise houses." A teacher on Port Royal Island described a praise house she visited. It was "a little chapel . . . made very roughly of boards whitewashed, inside an earth floor, covered with straw, rough wooden benches, the pulpit and altar made in the same way, but covered entirely with the grey moss."

Mose Hursey recounted the services he attended in the slave quarters. "On Sundays they had meetin', sometimes at our house, sometimes at 'nother house. They's preach and pray and sing—shout too. I heard them git up with a powerful force of the spirit, clappin' they hands and walkin' round the place. They's shout, 'I got the glory. I got that old time 'ligion in my heart.' I seen some powerful figurations of the spirit in them days."

Even in their own cabins and praise houses, bondsmen still felt their masters might be watching. In order to dance, pray, and serve God in their own way, they held late-night religious services deep in the woods.

The slaves were careful to keep these meetings secret from white people. "See, our masters didn't like us to have much 'ligion, said it made us lag in our work," explained a man in Louisiana, one of the few southern states where Roman Catholicism was common. "He jest wanted us to be Catholices [sic] on Sundays and go to mass and not study 'bout noth' like that on week days. He didn't want us shoutin' and moanin' all day long, but you gotta shout and you gotta moan if you wants to be saved."

Bondsmen frequently held prayer meetings after a long day of hard work. Under the watchful eye of the overseer, the workers in the cotton or tobacco fields might sing a certain song to alert others to a meeting. "When de niggers go round singin' 'Steal Away to Jesus,'" explained an old slave, "dat mean dere gwine be a 'ligious meetin' dat night." After the workday ended, usually at dusk, the faithful quietly slipped away to the "hush arbor," a meeting place hidden away in a gulley or grove of trees.

"Us niggers used to have a prayin' ground down in the hollow and sometime we come out of the field . . . scorchin' and burnin' up with nothin' to eat, and we wants to ask the good Lawd to have mercy," recalled former slave Richard Caruthers. "We takes a pine torch . . . and goes down in the hollow to pray. Some gits so joyous they starts to holler loud and we has to stop up they mouth. I see niggers git so full of the Lawd and so happy they draps unconscious."

The term "hush arbor" is a variation of "brush arbor." It probably came about because the worshipers had to be quiet so as not to attract patrollers. They tried several methods to hide the sounds of their clandestine meetings. Some worshipers hung up quilts soaked in water to muffle their prayers and songs. Or, in an unusual custom of unknown origin, slaves clustered around an upside-down iron kettle, believing their voices would be drawn into the kettle.

Several slave songs, such as "I Sought My Lord in de Wilderness," mention the hush arbor meetings.

I sought my Lord in de wilderness,
In de wilderness, in de wilderness;
I sought my Lord in de wilderness,
For I'm going home.

As I went down in de valley to pray,
Studying about dat good old way,

When you shall wear de starry crown,
Good Lord, show me the way.
O mourner, let's go down,
O mourner, let's go down,
Down in the valley to pray.

One of the favorite activities at the praise meetings was a shout, which whites disliked and even some blacks thought was too primitive. So people who enjoyed this trance-inducing dance had to do it secretly. And they made up songs—which they dubbed ring spirituals, running spirituals, or shout spirituals—to accompany their shouts.

Many spirituals evoked Christian images. While collecting songs on Port Royal Island, Colonel Higginson noticed that they often told stories from the Old Testament and the New Testament's Book of Revelation. These included stories of people saved by their faith in God, such as Jonah, who was swallowed by a whale; Daniel, who was thrown into the lion's den; and David, who slew the giant, Goliath, with a slingshot.

W.E.B. Du Bois, a founder of the National Association for the Advancement of Colored People (NAACP) and a college professor, explained why he thought spirituals, which he called sorrow songs, were so important to the slaves. "Through all of the Sorrow Songs there breathes a hope—a faith in the ultimate justice of things. The minor cadences of despair change often to triumph and calm confidence. Sometimes it is faith in life, sometimes a faith in death, sometimes assurance of boundless justice in some fair world beyond. But whichever it is, the meaning is always clear: that sometime, somewhere, men will judge men by their souls and not by their skins."

The Bible was a very important book among slaves. Illiterate African Americans learned about biblical characters, stories, and lessons from the songs they sang, from preachers' sermons, and from planters or their wives reading the Bible to them. Their knowledge of the Bible surprised many people.

Frederick Douglass, a Maryland slave until he escaped to freedom, said some spirituals encouraged bondsmen to flee. LIBRARY OF CONGRESS

"True, the most of them could not read, still, some of them line hymns from memory with great accuracy, and fervor, and repeat Scripture most appropriately, and correctly," observed the Reverend Mansfield French, one of the Gideonites. "One is amazed at their correctness and power."

The few slaves who could read often learned from the Bible. "Us poor niggers never allowed to learn anything," said W. L. Bost. "All the readin' they ever hear was when they was carried through the big Bible. . . . They was one nigger boy . . . who was terrible smart. He learnt to read and write. He take other colored children out in the fields and teach 'em about the Bible."

Slaves especially enjoyed biblical stories about the Children of Israel—the Jews—who were held in bondage by the pharaoh in Egypt until Moses led them to freedom. The old slave Mingo White explained why these stories were popular. "Somehow or yuther us had a instinct dat we was goin' to be free. . . . [W]hen de day's wuk was done de slaves would be foun' . . . in der cabins prayin' for de Lawd to free dem lack he did chillun of Is'ael."

African Americans expressed this feeling in one of their best-known spirituals, "Go Down, Moses."

> *Go down, Moses,*
> *Way down in Egypt land.*
> *Tell ole Pharaoh,*
> *Let my people go.*

During the Civil War slaves composed a similar song, which replaced Moses with Abraham Lincoln:

> *Oh! Fader Abraham,*
> *Go down into Dixie's land*
> *Tell Jeff Davis*
> *To let my people go.*
> *Down in the house of bondage*
> *Dey have watch and waited long,*
> *De oppressor's heel is heavy,*
> *De oppressor's arm is strong.*
> *Oh, Fader Abraham.*

The course of the Civil War, battles won and battles lost, was the subject of much discussion on southern plantations, among whites and bondsmen alike. "The old slaves told me that something was going on," recalled Thomas Rutling, a Tennessee slave, "and I must listen sharp up at the house, and come and tell them what the white folks said. . . . I was a table waiter then, and after talking over the news at table, missus would say, 'Now, Tom, you mustn't repeat a

Booker T. Washington, who was a slave until the age of nine, remembered that bondsmen on his plantation sang more enthusiastically at the end of the war, when they believed the North would win. LIBRARY OF CONGRESS

word of this.' I would look mighty obedient,—but—well—in less than half an hour, some way, every slave on the plantation would know what had been said up at massa's house.

"One would see sad faces when the Yankees got whipped, and then the preacher would have prayer meetings. I was too young to know what they prayed for, but heard the old slaves talking about freedom. By and by the rebels kept getting beaten, and then it was sing, sing, all through the slave quarters. Old missus asked what they were singing for, but they would only say, because we feel so happy."

Since they expressed so many of their feelings in songs, it is not surprising that slaves sang about the Civil War. "As the great day [of emancipation] grew nearer, there was more singing in the slave quarters than usual," said the educator Booker T. Washington, a former slave who had been a nine years old at the war's end. "It was bolder, had more ring, and lasted later into the night. Most of the verses of the plantation songs had some reference to freedom. True, they had sung those same verses before, but they had been careful to explain that the 'freedom' in these songs referred to the next world, and had no connection with life in this world. Now they gradually threw off the mask; and were not afraid to let it be known that the 'freedom' in their songs meant freedom of the body in this world."

He might have been referring to the popular song "Oh Freedom," which slaves composed in 1863, at about the same time that President Lincoln signed the Emancipation Proclamation.

> *Oh Freedom!*
> *Oh Freedom!*
> *Oh, freedom over me!*
> *And before I'd be a slave,*
> *I'll be buried in my grave,*
> *And go home to my Lord and be free!*

The Day of the Jubilee, or freedom, so often evoked in spirituals, arrived for all slaves when Robert E. Lee, commander of the Confederate army, surrendered at Appomattox, Virginia, on April 9, 1865. Finally free, black people were eager to discard all reminders of slavery days—including their music.

5

The First Black Singing Stars

Songs such as "Steal Away to Jesus" might have faded into obscurity except for the extraordinary talent of one small group of African Americans, the Fisk University Jubilee Singers, and their director, George Leonard White. By singing the old sorrow songs, the Jubilee Singers became one of the nineteenth century's most famous musical groups.

George White was born in 1838 and grew up in the western New York town of Franklinville, forty miles south of Buffalo. As a boy, George acquired a love of music from his father, a blacksmith and part-time musician.

When the Civil War started, George was twenty-two years old and a teacher in Ohio. He was among the thousands of Ohio men, called the Squirrel Hunters, who flocked to Cincinnati with their muskets to defend the city against Confederate attack. He then served in the Seventy-third Ohio regiment at the battles of Chancellorsville and Gettysburg in 1863. His regiment marched to Tennessee and fought the horrific battle of Lookout Mountain near Chattanooga. The following summer, illness forced the young soldier to quit the army.

White had recovered sufficiently by 1865 to take a job in the quartermaster's department in Nashville. As a teacher, he had once angered white neighbors in Ohio by organizing a Sunday school for local black children, and he had long been interested in working among African Americans. In Nashville he devoted his spare time to teaching penmanship and music to exslaves.

After Lee's surrender at Appomattox, White worked for the Freedmen's Bureau, a short-lived federal agency established to help the South's four million newly freed slaves, now called freedmen, obtain jobs, housing, and education. He married Laura Cravath in 1867. Shortly afterward her brother, Erastus Milo Cravath, the official in charge of Fisk, appointed White the school's treasurer.

White volunteered to be music director. Every evening he invited students to his home to sing and socialize. Sometimes the young people sang spirituals they had learned in the slave quarters. Ella Sheppard, a student, said her mother used to rock her to sleep singing "Swing Low, Sweet Chariot."

The music director began writing down and rearranging the words so they would appeal to modern audiences. "He was wonderful in the interpretation of those old Negro melodies," said one student, Georgia Gordon.

The American Missionary Association, the same organization that had sent teachers to Port Royal in 1862, had founded Fisk in 1866. At first it was called the Fisk Free Colored School. It was one of dozens of schools established by the A.M.A. to help educate the South's freedmen. There was at that time no state-supported education in the South, and many people believed these schools were essential to making freedmen self-reliant citizens.

Black people, both the young and the old, were eager to learn. "Lizzie Wilson was a slave for over fifty years," noted one teacher, "and has made such progress in reading as would suprise one unaccustomed to the zeal of these poor people." Booker T. Washington, who graduated from one of the new institutions, in Hampton, Virginia, remembered how important the schools were for freedmen. "Few people who were not right in the midst of the scene can

The original Fisk University occupied an old army hospital in downtown Nashville.
FISK UNIVERSITY LIBRARY'S SPECIAL COLLECTIONS

form an exact idea of the intense desire which the people of my race showed for an education. . . . It was a whole race trying to go to school."

Within a few months the Fisk Free Colored School had nearly one thousand students crowded into its makeshift classrooms. Fisk owned a cluster of twenty yellow buildings near the Cumberland River in downtown Nashville. The compound had been a hospital hastily built a few years earlier to treat wounded Union soldiers. The teachers, white men and women from the North, taught their classes in former sick wards and stored supplies in the former mortuary.

Late at night the students in the dormitories imagined they heard the groans of dying soldiers.

The school went through a number of changes in its first years. Many freedmen left the institution in 1867, when Tennessee began a statewide system of public schools. It changed its name several times before settling on Fisk University. Soon afterward Adam Spence, a University of Michigan professor, became the school's second president. He wanted to educate Fisk students, who now numbered fewer than one hundred, to become teachers who would staff the South's new black schools. But first the institution had to solve its financial problems.

By 1871 Fisk was so poor that students and faculty believed the school would have to close down. The wooden buildings were rotting away. Local merchants refused to provide goods until their bills were paid. Students were leaving to attend schools with better facilities. "There was no money even for food, much less for repairs. Many a time a special prayer was offered for the next meal," Ella Sheppard recalled.

The faculty and administrators talked wistfully of moving to a new campus, but the school lacked the money to buy land or construct buildings.

George White proposed a bold plan to raise money. He wanted to take the most talented members of his choir on a singing tour of northern states. Under White's direction the Fisk choir had achieved some local fame by performing in Atlanta and Memphis. In March 1871 he had produced a performance of *Esther, the Beautiful Queen* at Nashville's Masonic Hall, which raised three hundred dollars from an audience of black people, who had little money. This success convinced White that he could launch a profitable tour in Ohio and New York, where people were wealthier and interested in helping southern freedmen. To pay for expenses such as train tickets, hotel rooms, and meals, White wanted to use all the money in the school treasury.

Opposition was immediate. Some teachers, many of whom had not been paid for many months, argued that the school had more urgent needs for its meager funds. It was unlikely, they said, that a handful of students from a small Tennessee school could ever raise enough money to make the tour worthwhile. Others complained that their best students would miss many months of study. Parents objected to the tour because they feared for their children's safety.

People of all ages crowded the freedmen schools. LIBRARY OF CONGRESS

A group portrait of Fisk University teachers. George White is the tall man on the left in the back row. FISK UNIVERSITY LIBRARY'S SPECIAL COLLECTIONS

The decade following the Civil War was a violent and chaotic period in America's history known as Reconstruction. Southern whites fought the federal government's efforts to make exslaves equal citizens. Vigilante groups beat and murdered blacks. In 1866 white people in Memphis went on a three-day rampage, killing over forty freedmen while burning their homes, schools, and churches.

Despite the misgivings of parents and faculty members, White began choosing singers for the trip.

The Original Jubilee Singers

The lives of the first Jubilee Singers reflected the hardships black Americans endured both as slaves and as freedmen.

All four of the men—Greene Evans, Benjamin M. Holmes, Isaac P. Dickerson, and Thomas Rutling—had been born slaves. Thomas Rutling lost most of his large family when he was very young. "I may have been born out in the woods for ought [sic] I know," he once told an interviewer. "My mother was in the habit of running away and concealing herself in the woods, but she never remained long before she was found, brought back, and whipped. But whippings proved useless and she was sent further south. The very earliest thing that I remember was this selling of my mother. I must have been about two years old . . . when she kissed me and bade me goodby, and how she cried when they led her away."

Thomas described a similar fate for the rest of his family. "My father was sold before I was born and I know nothing of him. I had one brother, three or four years older than myself, and eight sisters. Some of my sisters were early sold away, and I do not know whether they are alive or not. . . . Once they talked of selling my brother, and I remember how hard he cried, how sorry we felt, though we were very small."

Benjamin M. Holmes, who was also separated from his family as a child, described how his parents in Charleston had encouraged him to read and write. State laws in the South forbade educating slaves, but they were difficult to enforce. Many slaves taught themselves basic reading and writing, and some masters taught favorite servants. "My father taught me my letters. In 1853, I was bound as an apprentice to Mr. Weston, a colored tailor. I was so small then I could hardly see over the bench. I studied all the signs and all the names on the doors where I carried bundles, and asked people to tell me a word or two at a time; til, in 1860, I found I could read the papers.

"My mother told me if I would learn to write she would give me a gold dollar. A part of my duty was to sweep the store in the morning, and I took some time to look in the measuring books to see how the writing letters were made. In this way I learned to write."

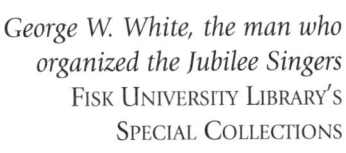
George W. White, the man who organized the Jubilee Singers
FISK UNIVERSITY LIBRARY'S SPECIAL COLLECTIONS

The man who owned Benjamin Holmes and his parents sold them in 1862 to a Charleston slave trader. "During the day we were kept in the slave mart, ready to be examined, and were fed upon cow's head, boiled grits, and rice. At night we were locked up." Benjamin remembered how news of the war spread quickly among the slaves, even reaching those locked up at the slave mart. "I read Lincoln's Proclamation in the prison. Such rejoicing as there was then! One man held a prayer meeting right there in the mart."

A Tennessee merchant purchased Benjamin and took him to Chattanooga to work in his store. When Union forces captured the city, the young man became the personal servant of Colonel Jefferson Columbia Davis. He accompanied Colonel Davis on General William T. Sherman's famous March to the Sea, the Union army's sweep in 1864 and early 1865 through Georgia and the Carolinas. By burning Atlanta, destroying important railroad lines, and laying waste to farms growing food for the Confederacy, Sherman hastened the end of the Civil War.

After the war Benjamin moved to Nashville to work for a barber. He enrolled in Fisk's primary department in 1868 but advanced to the high school division within two months.

Isaac P. Dickerson and Greene Evans also had both been in the war as teenage boys. Isaac was only eleven years old when the conflict began, and his master, J.F. Kent, a Virginia planter, joined the Confederate army as a colonel and took the boy along as a servant. Union soldiers captured Isaac, and he worked briefly for a northern officer until, homesick for his old master and friends, he slipped back to the Confederate lines.

After the war the ambitious former slave found a job in a Memphis store. The store owner's young son helped him learn to read and write. Dickerson also attended a local freedman's school until it was burned in the riot of 1866. The following year he taught in an all-black country school. Many of the teachers in these new schools were, like Isaac, only slightly better educated than their students.

Angry at not being paid, the young man taught only a few months before he resigned and moved to Nashville to enroll at Fisk.

Greene Evans was born on September 19, 1848, on a Fayette County plantation. His master, the richest man in that southwest Tennessee county, owned some fifty slaves. When the Union army invaded the state, the planter rounded up his slaves and fled to nearby Memphis and then south to Alabama. Greene became separated from the group. He found his way to the Union lines, and an officer hired the teenage boy as a servant. When the war ended, Greene returned to Memphis and found his family. Two years later he moved to Nashville to enroll at Fisk. He worked at the school painting, tending the grounds, and doing other maintenance work to pay his tuition.

When Greene left the university for a teaching job in southwestern Tennessee, he literally built the schoolhouse. The first classes were held outdoors while Greene, with help from his older students, cut down trees, split them into boards, and built a small school. Then he had to make the desks and benches for the students.

The women on the singing tour—Phebe Anderson, Maggie Porter, Eliza Walker, Jennie Jackson, Ella Sheppard, and Minnie Tate—ranged in age from fourteen to twenty. Little is known about two of the youngest girls, Phebe Anderson and Eliza Walker, both contraltos. Phebe was the only daughter of the Reverend Alfred Anderson, who was very protective. In one of his frequent letters to school officials, Reverend Anderson complained about the lack of heat in his daughter's dorm room. He also added that he did not want Phebe receiving love letters because "when marrying gets in the head there is no studying."

Fifteen-year-old Eliza Walker was a short, shy girl with braids framing her forehead. "I was born six miles from Nashville, at Flatrock in 1857," she told an interviewer. "My mother belonged to Wesley Greenfield and my father to John W. Walker of Nashville. There were eight children, two boys and six girls. I was next to the

The first Fisk Jubilee Singers, in 1871 Fisk University Library's Special Collections

youngest. My mistress held only two or three slaves besides our family. She finally set my mother free and gave her the three youngest children. After the war my father kept an ice house and made money enough to buy us a little home; but there was some trouble about the lease, and we lost the house. In 1866, I commenced attending Fisk School."

Although Jennie Jackson and Minnie Tate were both born before the Civil War, they were free blacks. "My grandfather was the slave and body servant of General Jackson," Jennie explained. "My mother's mistress set all her slaves free at her death, before my birth; so I was born free." Her grandfather, as slaves often did, took his owner's last name. In this case the name was well known. It was that of Andrew Jackson, the seventh president of the United States. Jackson owned one hundred fifty slaves on his plantation, Hermitage, near Nashville.

The black Jackson family, like most free blacks in the prewar South, struggled to earn a living. "I came to Nashville when three years old with my mother," Jennie said. "[I] lived with her till twelve or thirteen, when I hired as a nurse girl, at four dollars a month."

Jennie, a dark-skinned woman with soft features, attended school in Nashville during the war. "My mornings were spent at the wash-tub, and the afternoons in learning my letters; got so I could read in Easy Readings, then stopped, and did not return to school again till 1866, when I began at Fisk School."

It was there that Jennie discovered her strong and beautiful soprano voice. "I first began singing at Fisk School, and can remember how anxious I used to be to do well, and in my zeal often forgot where I was, when my teacher would say, 'That girl who sings so loud is making discords.'"

Minnie Tate, the troupe's third contralto, was fourteen and the youngest member. "I was born in Nashville, in 1857," she explained. "My parents were free. My mother was born in Mississippi, and when quite young her master died; but not till he had given free papers to my grandmother and some of her children."

Minnie said her grandmother wanted her family to grow up in a free state. "Taking all the worldly possessions they were able to carry in budgets [bags] on their heads, they started on foot, hardly realizing how far it was to free Ohio. They often had to rest on the way, and sometimes stopped for months in a place to earn money enough to make it safe for them to proceed."

The journey ended far short of Ohio, Minnie said. "At last they reached a German settlement in Tennessee. Here they were so well received and kindly treated that they decided to remain, well content to end their journey. My mother was sent to school with the white children, and really did not know but she was of as much account as any little girl.

"She soon began to turn her learning to some account by teaching other colored people. She taught all her children, and I can well remember my first lessons in our little home in Nashville. I have always been to school; but cannot think of any incidents in my own life that can be of particular interest to others."

Unlike Jennie and Minnie, soprano Maggie Porter was a slave the first twelve years of her life. She was born on February 2, 1853, in Lebanon, Tennessee. Her mother was a house servant for a planter who owned over two hundred slaves. Maggie grew up in her master's home, where, along with his children, she learned to read and write. When the war began, the planter took his house servants and moved to Nashville. At the end of the war, Maggie's mother, who was the head housekeeper, told the planter she wanted to be paid for her work. The man refused, so Mrs. Porter left to work for another family.

Maggie attended Fisk for two years before she took a job teaching in a one-room school in Bellevue, seventeen miles from Nashville. That first job ended suddenly during Christmas vacation 1868, when the Ku Klux Klan burned down her school. Maggie was one of George White's favorite singers. Although she was teaching in Murfreesboro, the music director asked her to sing the title role in his Nashville production of *Esther, the Beautiful Queen.*

Twenty-year-old Ella Sheppard, the third soprano, had her freedom purchased while she was an infant. "My father lived in Nashville, and had bought himself for $1800." Mr. Sheppard next tried to buy Ella and her mother, but their owner's wife refused to part with the older woman, who was a prized house servant. Ella's mother insisted that her daughter be sold to her husband, however, and he bought the infant for $350. Soon afterward Ella's mother was taken by her owners to Oklahoma. Mr. Sheppard purchased another woman's freedom for $1300 and married her.

Ella lived with her father and stepmother in Nashville until she was ten years old. "My father then kept a livery stable, and was doing quite a good business, owning four carriages and eight horses." But her father's business failed shortly after the war began. Mr. Sheppard had never formally filed papers of manumission, which would have made his wife and daughter legally free. When his creditors threatened to repossess them, the family fled to Cincinnati, Ohio.

The Sheppards lived in the black neighborhood called Ragtown. Ella attended the Seventh Street "colored school" and took piano lessons from a German lady. They had been in the city a year and a half when her father died suddenly of cholera. Ella had to stop her piano lessons and help her stepmother by working as a maid.

A family friend, perhaps knowing of Ella's talent, offered to pay for more music lessons. Ella studied voice with Madame Caroline Revé, who was embarrassed at having an African American student but welcomed the extra income. Ella was not allowed to reveal her teacher's name, and she had to go to Madame Revé's house after dark, so the neighbors would not see her.

When the war ended, Ella returned to Tennessee to teach in a black school in Gallatin, about twenty-five miles northeast of Nashville. The school was unable to pay her, and the young woman soon quit and moved to Nashville to attend Fisk. She taught music and sewed clothing to pay her expenses. At the end of her first year Ella was hired by White as assistant music teacher. She was the school's first black faculty member.

The Fisk students spent the summer of 1871 rehearsing. As fall approached, they must have felt a mixture of pride and anxiety. They could take pride in the fact that they had been chosen for such an important mission. But many of them must have worried that the future of Fisk University rested on their shoulders.

George White and his troupe set off on their journey early on the morning of October 6, 1871. President Spence gave White one thousand dollars to pay basic expenses. "Every dollar was raked and scraped to go," Spence lamented in a letter to his mother. "If money does not come in we will soon have nothing to eat."

The Northern Tour

The train carrying the Fisk singers arrived in Cincinnati late on October 6. They knew that before the war the river city had been a major stop for slaves fleeing the South on the secret Underground Railroad. And, like the people who had fled from bondage, the singers arrived in the Ohio city full of dreams. But none of them imagined that they were destined to become internationally known stars who sang for a president, a queen, and a king.

After checking into a hotel, they immediately went to a nearby exposition to perform. Ella Sheppard began by playing "Annie Laurie" on the piano. A curious crowd gathered, and one white observer pointed at Ella and exclaimed, "Do you see that? Do you hear that? Why, she's a nigger."

The crowd ignored the rude comment and listened attentively while the Fisk students sang such popular songs as "The Star-Spangled Banner," "Red, White, and Blue," "Away to the Meadows," "Old Folks at Home," and a temperance medley. The spectators applauded enthusiastically. The black singers were treated, a local writer observed, "with an admiration entirely new to these people, who, for many years, had no rights a white man was bound to respect."

During a typical performance the troupe sang as many as sixteen songs, which included a mix of popular and classical songs and perhaps two or three spirituals. Like other African Americans at the time, some of the Fisk students did not like to sing the work songs and spirituals of their parents and grandparents. "The slave songs," Ella believed, "were associated with slavery and the dark past, and represented the things to be forgotten."

The Fisk group performed at several Cincinnati churches, drawing large crowds but only small donations. After a few days they traveled farther north to other Ohio cities: Chillicothe, Springfield, Yellow Springs, Cleveland, and Oberlin.

In Chillicothe, two hotels turned the Fisk students away because of their race. A third, the American Hotel, rented them rooms

Poster advertising a performance in New York City FISK UNIVERSITY LIBRARY'S SPECIAL COLLECTIONS

Ella Sheppard with her younger sister in a photograph believed to have been taken in 1867 FISK UNIVERSITY LIBRARY'S SPECIAL COLLECTIONS

normally occupied by the staff, but they had to agree to avoid the dining room at mealtimes, when the white guests would be eating.

Such discrimination was commonplace, Maggie Porter remembered. "There were many times when we didn't have a place to sleep or anything to eat. Mr. White went out and bought us some sandwiches and tried to find some place to put us up."

The group became accustomed to this "caste prejudice," said Ella, "which was to follow us and which it was to be part of our mission if not to remove at least to ameliorate."

In late October the weather in Ohio turned frosty, and White had to spend most of the group's precious funds on warm clothing. Ella wore only cloth slippers on her feet. And Isaac Dickerson, an observer noted during the singer's first solo, dressed in "a rusty coat that was as much too long for the fashion as his trousers were too short for neighborly acquaintance with his shoes."

Minnie Tate was only fourteen at the beginning of the first tour. FISK UNIVERSITY LIBRARY'S SPECIAL COLLECTIONS

Reports of the group's hardships alarmed the students' parents back in Nashville. Phebe Anderson's father summoned his daughter home and made her promise never to go on tour again.

The group expected a warm reception in Oberlin. Many of Fisk's teachers had attended Oberlin College. The town had been a center of abolitionism before the Civil War and, like many of the other cities they visited, one of the stops on the Underground Railroad. In the 1850s, a time when few people attended college, Oberlin counted over two hundred African Americans among its graduates. It was in this college town that White and his troupe began to understand the broad appeal that spirituals had beyond the black community.

On November 16, 1871, the remaining nine students sat in the balcony at Oberlin's First Church while the National Congregational Council conducted a business meeting on the main floor below. During a break in the meeting, the group quietly stood and began singing "Steal Away to Jesus."

> *Steal away, steal away, steal away to Jesus!*
> *Steal away, steal away home,*
> *I hain't got long to stay here.*
> *My Lord calls me, He calls me by the thunder;*
> *The trumpet sounds it in my soul,*
> *I hain't got long to stay here.*

They started very softly and grew louder as the surprised ministers stopped talking and looked up at the balcony. At the end of the song the ministers broke into loud applause and called for more. The songs, one man wrote, were "richly melodious and showed that analogy between the feeling of the slaves at the South and that of the captive Israelites." They took up a collection that "resulted in a market basket full of scrip and greenbacks." This enthusiasm persuaded White to add more spirituals to their performances. Soon the group sang nothing else but spirituals, and the old sorrow songs made them famous.

White worried that his group did not have a name. The newspapers often called them Colored Christian Singers—or minstrels, a term they especially disliked. Minstrels were popular entertainers in that era. Some were African American, but most were white people who blackened their faces with burnt cork and sang old plantation songs while portraying blacks as comic figures to be ridiculed.

White chose the name Jubilee Singers because he liked the lyrical sound and because it was "in memory of the Jewish year of

Poster advertising a minstrel show LIBRARY OF CONGRESS

Jubilee." This was a biblical reference to a time when Jewish slaves in Egypt were set free. In the Old Testament, White explained, "the 'Year of Jubilee' had always been the favorite figure of speech into which the [American] slaves put their prayers and hopes for emancipation."

Despite their success at Oberlin, donations were still small, and the discouraged students felt they would never make enough money to help Fisk University. They were tired of being turned away from hotels and restaurants. And the places where they did stay were often unpleasant. One hotel room, Ella reported, was so infested with bugs "that a part of us only could sleep while the others slew the occupants." The singers talked about giving up and returning to Nashville. "Our strength was failing under the ill treatment at hotels, on railroads, poorly attended concerts and ridicule," Ella explained. But they decided that they should at least go as far as New York.

The Jubilee Singers traveled to Elmira, New York, to sing at the Reverend Thomas K. Beecher's First Presbyterian Church. Their music so impressed Reverend Beecher that he wrote an enthusiastic letter to his brother, the Reverend Henry Ward Beecher, suggesting the group perform at his church in Brooklyn, New York.

Henry Ward Beecher was an eloquent speaker and the most famous preacher in America. He had been a prominent abolitionist before the Civil War. Hatred of slavery seemed to run in the family. His sister, Harriet Beecher Stowe, wrote *Uncle Tom's Cabin*, a novel about the evils of slavery. When the book was published in 1852, it was banned in the South and widely read in the North. Historians have called it "the most powerful of all abolitionist propaganda." President Abraham Lincoln once joked that Beecher's novel caused the Civil War.

Reverend Beecher's fame had drawn many wealthy and influential families to his Plymouth Congregational Church in Brooklyn. They filled the pews the day the Jubilee Singers performed. The group sang several lively spirituals that made Reverend Beecher laugh "till the tears rolled down his cheeks." Afterward he made a great show of opening his purse and extracting money. He told his congregation to "do likewise. Folks can't live on air. Though they sing like nightingales, they need more to eat than nightingales do."

Several newspapers published snide, sarcastic articles that reflected the blatant racism so common then. "Now this is precious humbug," a *New York Herald* reporter wrote, "to see all of these people come here and patronize these poor niggers, who ought to be home in their beds."

But fans of the singers responded to the newspaper articles with long, eloquent letters. "I never saw a cultivated Brooklyn assemblage so moved and melted under the magnetism of music before," wrote Theodore Ledyard Cuyler, the pastor of Brooklyn's Lafayette Avenue Presbyterian Church, to *The New York Tribune*. "The wild melodies of these emancipated slaves touched the fount of tears, and gray haired men wept like little children. . . . Allow me to bespeak a universal welcome through the North for these living representatives of the only true native school of American music. . . . Our people can now listen to the genuine soul music of the slave cabins before the Lord led his children out of the land of Egypt and out of the house of bondage."

The performance at Reverend Beecher's church was a turning point for White's troupe. "I think the collection was two hundred and fifty dollars," Maggie Porter reported. "That was our start. Every church wanted the Jubilee Singers to sing for them. . . . From that time on we had success." Just a few weeks later White proudly sent six hundred dollars to President Spence at Fisk. In the accompanying note the music director confidently predicted, "Success is sure. It is only a matter of time."

The Jubilee Singers performed to full auditoriums and churches in Brooklyn and across the East River in Manhattan. White no longer had to ask for donations after each concert. He sold tickets, and the group earned as much as seven hundred dollars a night.

Their fame spread throughout the Northeast. "They will charm any audience," Brooklyn's Reverend Beecher wrote to a Boston friend. "They make their mark by giving the 'spirituals' and plantation hymns as only they can sing them who know how to keep time to a master's whip. Our people have been delighted."

That winter the Jubilee Singers toured New England and New York, Pennsylvania, and New Jersey. The gave concerts nearly every evening and sometimes during the day as well. Mark Twain, who lived in Hartford, Connecticut, heard them and said, "I do not know when anything has so moved me as did the plaintive melodies of the Jubilee Singers."

Despite their fame the Jubilees still met with frequent discrimination. Hotels in both New Haven, Connecticut, and Newark, New Jersey, turned them away. But it was encouraging that prominent citizens in both cities invited the singers into their homes. "By their sweet songs and simple ways," noted the *New Jersey Journal*, the group was "molding and manufacturing public sentiment."

The troupe visited Washington, D.C., in March 1872 to perform at Howard University. While they were in the nation's capital, President Ulysses S. Grant invited them to sing at the White House. He asked the group to sing "Go Down, Moses."

When Israel was in Egypt's land,
Let my people go,
Oppressed so hard they could not stand,
Let my people go.
Go down, Moses,
Way down in Egypt land,
Tell ole Pharaoh,
Let my people go.

By the following month the Jubilee Singers had earned over twenty thousand dollars. It was time to go home. Only one incident marred their trip. While they were changing trains in Louisville, Kentucky, a cursing policeman chased the young men and women from a "whites only" waiting room. Railroad officials heard of the incident and put the group on a luxurious Pullman rail car for the rest of their trip.

In Nashville, Fisk students and faculty, beating drums and waving flags, greeted the returning Jubilee Singers as if they were victorious soldiers returning home from battle.

The money they had earned enabled Fisk to pay all its debts as well as buy land for a new campus. One of the first buildings constructed on the new campus was named Jubilee Hall. School officials said it had been "sung up" by the Jubilee Singers. Soon after construction began, the group embarked on its first European tour.

Singing for Royalty

In April 1873 the Jubilee Singers sailed across the Atlantic Ocean and, after eleven days at sea, arrived in England. George White carried letters of introduction from Reverend Henry Ward Beecher and Mark Twain. The group received a grand welcome in London.

The Earl of Shaftesbury organized the Jubilees' first performance on May 6 at Willis's Rooms on Grosvenor Square. An audience of some six hundred aristocrats eager to see newly emancipated slaves filled the room. There were thirteen Jubilees on this tour. Eight of the original members had been joined by five new ones. They stood three deep on a platform, looked slightly upward as if seeking inspiration from heaven, and began with their signature song, "Steal Away to Jesus." One Englishman described hearing the song for the first time:

"It was sung slowly; the first chords came floating on our senses like gentle fairy music, and they were followed by unison of phrase, 'Steal Away—to Jesus,' delivered with exquisite precision of time and accent; then came the soft chords and bold unison again followed by the touching, throbbing cadence, 'I hain't got long to stay here,' next followed the loud, lofty trumpet call in unison, 'My lord calls me, the trumpet sounds it in my soul; I hain't got long to stay here.' But it seems as though the angels also were speaking to the sufferer for we hear again those beautiful chords delivered with double pianis-simo, whispering to the soul, 'Steal Away to Jesus.'"

The rest of the program included "Gwine Ride Up in the Char-iot" and "Turn Back Pharaoh's Army." This last song alternated from solo to a fast chorus:

> *Gwine to write to Massa Jesus,*
> *To send some valiant soldier,*
> *To turn back Pharaoh's army, Hallelujah!*
> *To turn back Pharaoh's army, Hallelujah!*
> *To turn back Pharaoh's army, Hallelujah!*
> *To turn back Pharaoh's army, Hallelujah!*
> *If you want your souls converted,*
> *You'd better be a-praying . . .*

"We captured the hearts of the Englishmen," reported Georgia Gordon, one of the new members of the group. "We sang ourselves into their very souls. We could hear 'Bravo! Hear! Hear!' their way of expressing approval."

The Duke and Duchess of Argyll were in the audience and invited White's troupe to perform the next day at their mansion. The fol-lowing day at Argyll Lodge, the singers were surprised by an un-expected guest, Queen Victoria. The duke summoned the surprised and nervous performers to a private room occupied by the queen and her entourage.

Victoria was fifty-three years old, short and stout. She was still in mourning for her husband, Prince Albert, who had died twelve years earlier. She wore a black velvet dress and a string of large pearls around her neck.

Her majesty's ordinariness surprised Maggie Porter. "I received the greatest disappointment of my life. The queen wore no crown, no robes of state. She was like many English ladies I had seen in her widow's cap and weeds. But it was the queen in flesh and blood.".

Victoria did not speak directly to the Fisk singers. She studied

A painting depicting the Jubilee Singers performing for Queen Victoria in May 1873
Fisk University Library's Special Collections

them as they filed into the room. When the singers were assembled, the duke relayed the queen's request. The Jubilees sang "Steal Away to Jesus," and "Go Down, Moses," and chanted the Lord's Prayer. Afterward her Majesty neither clapped nor smiled. But Victoria later noted in her journal that the Jubilees "sing extremely well together."

After their successful London debut, the singers spent nearly a year touring England, Ireland, and Scotland. They performed for more aristocrats and gave numerous free concerts at churches, revivals, orphanages, and temperance meetings. Tens of thousands of people heard the African Americans sing the old sorrow songs of their ancestors.

This tour was very different from their first journey two years earlier through the northeastern United States. They rode in first-class train cars, slept in luxurious hotels, and dined in expensive restaurants. Admirers showered them with gifts, such as jewelry and clothing. Hopeful suitors sought the attention of the women. The singers were now professionals earning five hundred dollars a year, which was more than a teacher at Fisk earned.

The group had grown more confident. They readily expressed their opinions about schedules and accommodations. Several of the men discussed remaining in Europe and touring on their own. Such talk angered George White, who called it disloyal. White was fond of referring to the singers as "his children," and he had difficulty accepting their growing independence. He expressed his displeasure in a letter to his brother-in-law: "Most of the singers remain humble, but a few give me infinite trouble."

In early 1874 fatigue caused by constant traveling and performing, combined with the cold and damp winter weather of the British Isles, made several members of the group ill. The most seriously affected was Laura White.

She had accompanied her husband, thinking the trip would be fun and restful. But Laura was constantly bedridden with headaches and back pain. While in Scotland in February, she caught typhoid fever and died. Her husband was distraught, and his health also began to deteriorate. He coughed up blood and was bedridden for weeks. His faithful protégée, Ella Sheppard, took over the job of rehearsing and directing the troupe. When they boarded their ship to sail for home, White had to be carried on a mattress.

Financially the tour of the British Isles was a great success. The trip raised eleven thousand pounds, which was equivalent at that time to fifty thousand American dollars. The money helped Fisk University build its new campus in Nashville.

The Jubilee Singers returned to Europe the following year. They sang in Holland's cathedrals and earned high praise in Germany, a country

Benjamin Holmes in Edinburgh, Scotland, in 1873 FISK UNIVERSITY LIBRARY'S SPECIAL COLLECTIONS

famous for its composers and musicians. They performed for Frederick the Great, the King of Prussia. And in Edinburgh, Scotland's capital and a city of half a million people, officials gave the Jubilee Singers a grand welcoming celebration normally reserved for visiting dignitaries.

Back home in America their success inspired other black schools to form similar traveling vocal groups. Sixteen students from Hampton University, a freedmen's school in eastern Virginia, set out in February 1873 on a singing tour that raised seventy-five thousand dollars. Hampton officials used the money to build a chapel, dining room,

Thomas Rutling in Manchester, England, in 1874 FISK UNIVERSITY LIBRARY'S SPECIAL COLLECTIONS

and dormitory. Within just a few years dozens of groups—such as Atlanta's Morehouse College Singers and Alabama's Tuskegee University choir—were crisscrossing the country and singing the old spirituals for large audiences.

While most of the original Jubilees had lifelong careers as singers, a few chose different paths.

Greene Evans, who had developed his public-speaking skills as a member of Fisk's literary club, dropped out of the second Jubilee tour and moved to Memphis, where he entered politics. He was elected to the Memphis City Council and then to Tennessee's general assembly.

At the end of the Jubilees' first tour of the British Isles, in 1874, Isaac Dickerson accepted an offer to attend the University of Edinburgh, where he earned a degree in divinity. He spent several years preaching, singing, and bicycling through France, Germany, and Palestine. Dickerson settled in London to work as a missionary in that city's slums. He died there in 1900.

Thomas Rutling left the group after the Jubilees' second European tour. He hiked through Switzerland, Germany, and Italy before moving to England, where he worked as a singer and voice teacher. He died in that country in 1915.

Jennie Jackson and Maggie Porter sang for Fisk University until the late 1870s. They then joined Minnie Tate and several other singers for an around-the-world tour that lasted over six years. Although no longer affiliated with Fisk, they called themselves the Jubilee Singers. They performed in the British Isles, Australia, New Zealand, India, Hong Kong, and Japan.

Afterward, Porter formed a group called the Original Fisk Jubilee Singers. The black singers encountered so much discrimination in the old Confederate states that she moved to Detroit and vowed never to return to the South again. Jackson also organized her own troupe. Using her married name, she called her group the Jennie Jackson Dehart Jubilee Club.

Jubilee Hall at Fisk University, which was constructed with money raised by the Jubilee Singers FISK UNIVERSITY LIBRARY'S SPECIAL COLLECTIONS

Ella Sheppard married George Washington Moore in the parlor of George White's home in 1882, three days before Christmas. The couple lived in Washington, D.C., for nearly a decade before returning to Nashville. Ella used the money she had earned singing to build a home near the Fisk University campus. Some years earlier she had found her mother, Sara, in Oklahoma, and she brought the elderly woman back to Nashville. It was the first time since they had been slaves that mother and daughter had shared a home. Ella performed publicly for the last time in 1913, a year before she died, and sang "Swing Low, Sweet Chariot."

George White, the man who created the Jubilee Singers, profited little from the group's success. On the second European tour he abruptly resigned over disagreements with several of the singers and with Fisk's president. Back in the United States he organized a new group called the Jubilees, which had no affiliation with Fisk. The Jubilees toured from 1879 to 1882, when, suffering again from ill health, White retired from music. He and his second wife, Susan, moved to Fredonia, New York. White's health became so bad that he was unable to work, and Susan had to take a job as a housekeeper. He died in 1895.

Fisk University, now well over a century old, has a large campus in Nashville. Its graduates include such distinguished people as scholar W.E.B. Du Bois, poet James Weldon Johnson, writer Arna Bontemps, singer Roland Hayes, historian John Hope Franklin, and children's book author Julius Lester.

Today the Jubilee Singers are remembered not only for helping to save Fisk from bankruptcy but also for introducing the world to slave spirituals. Those sacred songs, which celebrated the indomitable human spirit, are still inspiring people in America and throughout the world.

In Charleston, South Carolina, in 1945 black tobacco workers engaged in a bitter labor strike changed the words to "I Shall Overcome," an old Sea Island spiritual, to "We Shall Overcome," making it a rallying song for the strikers.

Civil rights workers in the 1960s sang this song, along with other spirituals, when they faced violent crowds in their protests against segregation. Dr. Martin Luther King Jr. and his fellow protesters liked the song so much that it became the anthem for the civil rights movement. And halfway around the world in South Africa, Bishop Desmond Tutu, a leader in that country's antiapartheid movement, observed that the old spiritual expressed a feeling black South Africans readily understood. "When we sing 'We Shall Overcome,' what we will overcome is injustice, is apartheid, is separation—all that is dehumanizing."

Source Notes

Foreword
Eileen Southern's *The Music of Black Americans* traces the development of African American music from African call and response to modern-day hip hop. The James Weldon Johnson quotation is from the preface to his first collection of spirituals. The poet and writer teamed up with his composer brother, J. Rosamond Johnson, in the 1920s to edit two collections, *The Book of American Negro Spirituals* (1925) and *The Second Book of Negro Spirituals* (1926). Years earlier, in 1900, the Florida-born brothers composed *Lift Every Voice*, a gospel song that became so popular among African Americans that it was called the Black National Anthem.

1   Strange and Beautiful Songs
Chapter 1 relies on two firsthand accounts of life in the Sea Islands during the Civil War: Charlotte L. Forten's *The Journal of Charlotte Forten* (New York: Oxford, 1989) and Thomas Wentworth Higginson's autobiographical *Army Life in a Black Regiment* (New York: Norton, 1984). Historical background is provided by Willie Lee Rose's *Rehearsal for Reconstruction: The Port Royal Experiment* (New York: Oxford, 1964).

2   Musical Africa
This chapter is based on information from John Lovell Jr.'s *Black Song: The Forge and the Flame* (New York: Macmillan, 1972); Robert Palmer's *Deep Blues: A Musical and Cultural History of the Mississippi Delta* (New York: Penguin, 1985); Marshall Stearns's *The Story of Jazz* (New York: Oxford, 1958); and Southern's *The Music of Black Americans.*

3   Slave Music
Chapter 3 relies on Lawrence W. Levine's monumental *Black Culture and Black Consciousness*; John W. Blassingame's *The Slave Community: Plantation Life in the*

Antebellum South (New York: Oxford, 1975); Peter Kolchin's *American Slavery 1619–1877* (New York: Hill & Wang, 1993); Booker T. Washington's *Up from Slavery* (New York: Dover Publications, 1998); John Hope Franklin's *From Slavery to Freedom: A History of African Americans* (New York: Knopf, 2000); and Southern's *The Music of Black Americans.*

4   *The Secret Church*
The primary source for this chapter is Albert J. Raboteau's *Slave Religion: The "Invisible Institution" in the Antebellum South* (New York: Oxford, 1990). The long quotation about sorrow songs is from W.E.B. Du Bois's *The Souls of Black Folk* (New York: Dutton, 1995); additional information comes from Levine's *Black Culture and Black Consciousness*, Franklin's *From Slavery to Freedom*, and Southern's *The Music of Black Americans.*

5   *The First Black Singing Stars*
The Jubilee Singers and Their Campaign for Twenty Thousand Dollars by Gustavus D. Pike (Boston: Lee and Shepard, 1873) and his *The Singing Campaign for Ten Thousand Pounds: or, The Jubilee Singers in Great Britain* (Freeport, N.Y.: Books for Libraries, 1971) are both accounts written by the Jubilee Singers' booking agent. Additional source notes include *The New Grove Dictionary of Music and Musicians*, Stanley Sadie, ed. (New York: Macmillan, 1982), and John Lovell Jr.'s *Black Song.*

6   *The Original Jubilee Singers*
The best source for information on the Jubilees and their times is Andrew Ward's *Dark Midnight When I Rise*. Arna Bontemps, who attended Fisk, wrote a fictionalized account of the Jubilee Singers, *Chariot in the Sky.*

7   *The Northern Tour*
Ward's *Dark Midnight When I Rise* is a very good, balanced account of the group, while Pike's *The Jubilee Singers* is an effusive description of the singers.

8   *Singing for Royalty*
Pike's *The Singing Campaign for Ten Thousand Pounds* covers the British and European tours, but Ward's *Dark Midnight When I Rise* is a better source.

Further Reading

Bontemps, Arna. *Chariot in the Sky: A Story of the Jubilee Singers* (New York: Holt, Rinehart & Winston, 1971).

Hopkinson, Deborah. *A Band of Angels: A Story Inspired by the Jubilee Singers* (New York: Atheneum, 1999). Ages 6 to 9.

Levine, Lawrence W. *Black Culture and Black Consciousness: Afro-American Folk Thought from Slavery to Freedom* (New York: Oxford, 1978).

Southern, Eileen. *The Music of Black Americans* (New York: Norton, 1997).

Ward, Andrew. *Dark Midnight When I Rise: The Story of the Jubilee Singers* (New York: Farrar, Straus and Giroux, 2000).

Seven Slave Spirituals—
Words and Music

Colonel Thomas Wentworth Higginson was not the only person in the Sea Islands writing down slave spirituals during the Civil War. Three missionaries, William Francis Allen, Charles Pickard Ware, and Lucy McKim Garrison, also collected spirituals. They published their collection in 1867 in a book titled *Slave Songs of the United States*. They described the first song in their book, "Roll, Jordan, Roll," as "one of the noblest and best known of the slave spirituals."

Although *Slave Songs of the United States* was the first bound volume of spirituals, a few individual songs had been published previously. According to *The Book of World Famous Music* (New York: Dover Publications, 1995), "Go Down, Moses" was "the first still well-known Negro spiritual to have appeared in print."

The people who collected and published slave spirituals helped save them for future generations, but it was the Fisk Jubilee Singers who made the music popular. "Steal Away," "Swing Low, Sweet Chariot," and "Sweet Canaan" are just three of the many spirituals the Jubilee Singers sang for audiences in America and Europe.

Before I'd Be a Slave

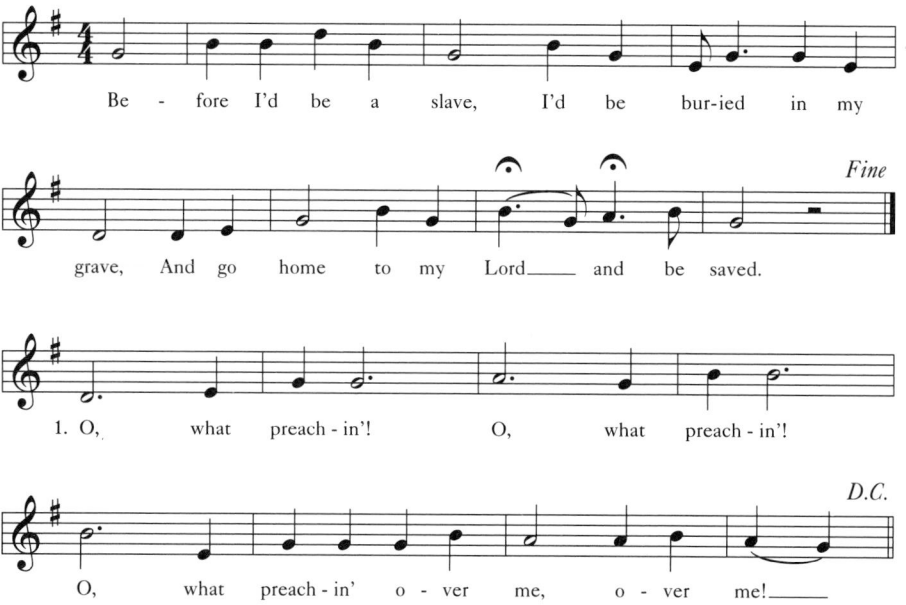

Before I'd be a slave, I'd be bur-ied in my grave, And go home to my Lord___ and be saved.

Fine

1. O, what preach-in'! O, what preach-in'!

D.C.

O, what preach-in' o - ver me, o - ver me!___

2. O, what mourning, etc.
3. O, what singing, etc.
4. O, what shouting, etc.
5. O, weeping Mary, etc.
6. Doubting Thomas, etc.
7. O, what sighing, etc.

Go Down, Moses

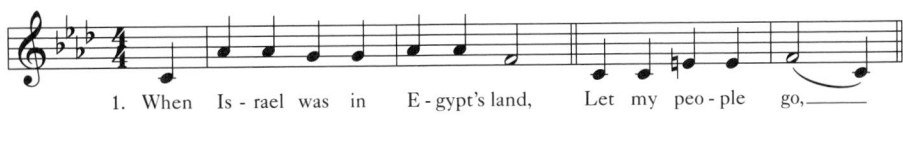

1. When Is - rael was in E - gypt's land, Let my peo - ple go,____

Op - pressed so hard they could not stand, Let my peo - ple go,

Go down, Mo - ses, way down in E - gypt land,__

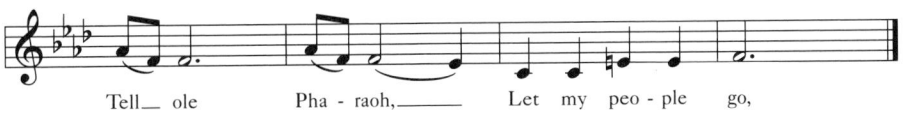

Tell__ ole Pha - raoh,_____ Let my peo - ple go,

2. Thus saith the Lord, bold Moses said,
   Let my people go,
   I not I'll smite your firstborn dead,
   Let my people go.
   Go down, Moses, etc.

3. Nor more shall they in bondage toil,
   Let my people go,
   Let them come out with Egypt's spoil,
   Let my people go,
   Go down, Moses, etc.

4. When Israel out of Egypt came,
   Let my people go,
   And left the proud oppressive land,
   Let my people go.
   Go down, Moses, etc.

Michael, Row the Boat Ashore

1. Mich-ael, row de boat a-shore, Hal-le-lu - jah!

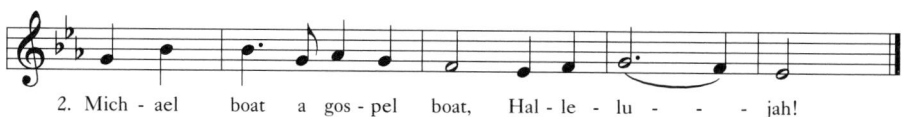

2. Mich-ael boat a gos-pel boat, Hal-le-lu - - jah!

3. I wonder were my mudder deh [there]
4. See my mudder on de rock gwine home.
5. On de rock gwine home in Jesus' name.
6. Michael boat a music boat.
7. Gabriel blow de trumpet horn.
8. O you mind your boastin' talk.
9. Boastin' talk will sink your soul.
10. Brudder, lend a helpin' hand.
11. Sister, help for trim dat boat.
12. Jordan stream is wide and deep.
13. Jesus stand on t' oder side.
14. I wonder if my maussa deh.
15. My fader gone to unknown land.
16. O de Lord he plant his garden deh.

Nobody Knows the Trouble I See, Lord

No-bo-dy knows the trou-ble I see, Lord, No-bo-dy knows the

trou-ble I see, No-bo-dy knows the trou-ble I see, Lord,

Fine

No-bo-dy knows like Je - sus. 1. Broth - ers, will you

pray for me, Broth-ers, will you pray for me, Broth-ers, will you

D.C.

pray for me And help me to drive old Sa - tan a - way.

2. Sisters, will you pray for me, etc.

3. Mothers, will you pray for me, etc.

4. Preachers, will you pray for me, etc.

Roll, Jordan, Roll

1. My brud-der sit-tin' on de tree of life, An' he year-de when Jor-dan roll;_____ Roll, Jor-dan, Roll, Jor-dan, Roll, Jor-dan, roll! O march de an-gel march, O march de an-gel march; O my soul a-rise in Heav-en, Lord, For to year-de when Jor-dan roll.

2. Little chil'en, learn to fear de Lord,
   And let your days be long ;
   Roll, Jordan, etc.
3. O, let no false nor spiteful word
   Be found upon your tongue ;
   Roll, Jordan, etc.

Steal Away

Steal a-way, Steal a-way, Steal a-way to Je-sus!

Steal a-way, Steal a-way home, I hain't got long to stay here.

Fine

1. My Lord____ calls me, He calls me by the thun-der; The

trum-pet sounds it in my soul,— I hain't got long to stay here.

D.C.

2. Green trees are bending, poor sinners stand trembling;
    The trumpet sounds it in my soul, —
  I hain't got long to stay here.
        Steal away, etc.

3. My Lord calls me, He calls me by the lightning;
    The trumpet sounds it in my soul,—
  I hain't got long to stay here.
        Steal away, etc.

4. Tombstones are bursting, poor sinners stand trembling ;
    The trumpet sounds it in my soul,—
  I hain't got long to stay here.
        Steal away, etc.

Swing Low, Sweet Chariot

Swing low, sweet char - i - ot,___ Com-ing for to car - ry me home.

Fine

Swing low, sweet char - i - ot,___ Com-ing for to car-ry me home.

1. I looked o - ver Jor - dan, and what did I see,___

Com-ing for to car - ry me home? A band__ of an - gels

D.C.

com-ing af - ter me,___ Com-ing for to car - ry me home.

2. If you get there before I do, Coming for to carry me home,
   Tell all my friends I'm coming too, Coming for to carry me home.
      Swing low, etc.
3. The brightest day that ever I saw, Coming for to carry me home,
   When Jesus washed my sins away, Coming for to carry me home.
      Swing low, etc.
4. I'm sometimes up and sometimes down, Coming for to carry me home,
   But still my soul feels heavenly bound, Coming for to carry me home.
      Swing low, etc.

Index

Page numbers in **bold** type refer to illustrations.